Waves Of Blue Light

Waves Of Blue Light

Heal the Heart and Free the Soul

M.J. Domet

To order additional copies of this book, contact:
Xlibris Corporation
1-888-795-4274
www.Xlibris.com
Orders@Xlibris.com
93163

To My Family—Don, David, Lisa, and Lexi
I Love You.
And to Teri, Joe, and Mike
You will always be family because you love mine.

Introduction

I usually tell people that I began my search for truth later in life, but it really began many lifetimes ago and has cumulated to this point in time of March 2011. The consciousness I have received as a result of my explorations has led me to help other people with their own journeys.

Assisting them, my understanding and awareness of my own path has increased along with the added blessing of having many people in my circle who were not there at the beginning of this life adventure.

I am truly honoured by each individual's presence in my life. Every one of you has taught me something, which has given me additional knowledge to work with every step of my way.

I have so many people I could mention by name, but it would take up many pages of this book, so I hope you will all recognise yourselves as part of one or more of these groups: I want to thank my family and friends as you are my first teachers; my clients and students, who are such an inspiration to me in the work I do; my spiritual teachers, thank you for your wisdom; the monthly Reiki and Deep Healing Groups, which have helped me immensely in clearing emotional residue in order for this, my first book, to be completed; and as always, to my spirit guides who are cheering as I write this. I love you all!

I am as honest about my life within this work as possible, and any feelings I express are genuine impressions of how I felt at the time of the lesson. Knowing that my experiences have led me to this moment, I do not hold any judgements around any person or incident contained within these pages, including myself. I know that healing does not occur unless you are willing to see a new perspective or gain insight around the meaning of the experience. I often refer to the modalities of Reiki and Deep Cellular Healing. These are energy works that have been instrumental in bringing me to this point in my life. Through using them, I have released major emotional, spiritual, and physical issues, which I once thought to be unshakable elements in my life.

As you go through the affirmations at the end of each section, please remember to breathe each statement in and release your breath to completely accept the new belief and release the outdated, redundant view.

My wish is for this work to help you progress on your own path to spiritual enlightenment as I want to give back to you at least as much as I have received.

Embrace the journey and carry on with all the passion you can muster. You never know what you will encounter, and that is the best reason of all to continue.

Expect to be empowered!

With love-n-light,
MJ (Marilyn)

Belief creates endless possibilities.

After several years of working as a healing facilitator, I began to see a beautiful blue light when assisting clients. This light is a strikingly vivid colour that is difficult to describe as I have never seen anything like it, except when providing or receiving energy healing.

The light comes from a place other than my physical self. It flows through me as a gift from Spirit as the light becomes me and I it. There is no separation; its strength courses through me with an intensity that is beyond time, space, and physical limitation. The less I try to control it and the more I permit it to do what it is meant to, the more healing it promotes.

The power of the light depends on my willingness to allow it to take over. When I do, without fear, I realise we are working as one to restore wholeness either individually or with a group of people.

The blue energy did not materialise until I reached the level of awareness that accompanies its emergence. Before getting to the point of accepting the potential of this healing force, my life was very different. I had a few difficult lessons to learn and issues to work through prior to helping others. Many of these events will be revealed throughout the inspirational pages and poetry in this book.

Although having always been interested in composing poetry and dabbling in it a bit, I was only able to immerse myself totally in writing when I was spiritually ready to combine it with life lessons.

That is my inspiration!

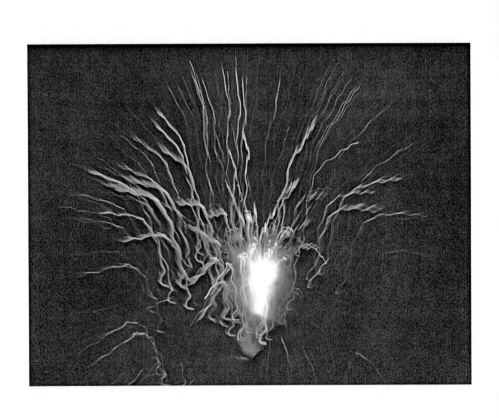

The Light

Energy moves around me with pulsating blue waves
Tiny points of light swirling with increasing intensity.
Welcoming the light,
I know—I am the light.

I am moving in perfect rhythm with the vibration
Its illuminating beams dancing about my physical being.
As I accept the light,
I know—I am the light.

Accentuating and highlighting, the vivid colour bombards me
It creates a tingling that immerses me in the power completely.
As I acknowledge the light,
I know—I am the light.

The sensation of this force overwhelms me
Leaving me feeling completely vital and whole.
As I recognise the light,
I know—I am the light.

Swiftly as the power engulfs my body, mind, and soul,
It energises me to a complete understanding.
As I believe in the light,
I become the light.

Light Affirmations

1. My body, mind, and soul recognise the light within me.
2. I allow my body, mind, and soul to be guided by the loving light energy.
3. I embrace the light, filling my body, mind, and soul with the energy of universal oneness.
4. As I receive the light, my body, mind, and soul release the negative results of fear, which have prohibited my spiritual growth.
5. The light promotes my understanding of universal, unconditional love.
6. My body, mind, and soul are empowered by the strength of love emanating from the light.
7. I welcome the light, letting its knowledge penetrate my body, mind, and soul.
8. As I open up to the knowledge within me, my body, mind, and soul become one.
9. I open my body, mind, and soul up to universal wisdom and acknowledge all that I am.
10. The light completes my understanding of my spiritual journey, allowing my body, mind, and soul to fulfil the purpose of connecting me to the source.
11. As my heart receives the light, I feel at peace knowing I am always loved.
12. My body, mind, and soul realise that I am and will forever be an integral part of the light.

> ## Walk your path with confidence knowing support will be there every step of the way.

I became a Reiki Master Teacher a few years ago in three disciplines. Before being introduced to the energy, I had never heard of Reiki. It is amazing how things come to you in the right time and right place!

After finishing the first four levels of Usui Reiki, I went on to the advanced modalities of Karuna and Komyo. Beginning this spiritual journey later in life inspired me to complete all three Reiki disciplines in less than two years and was the motivation I needed to help me progress quickly on my path.

I had given up my profession as a preschool teacher two years earlier, as it just didn't seem right for me anymore. All the joy was gone. Although I loved being with the children, feeling burnt out, I felt as if I just didn't have any more to contribute in that area.

I had known it was time for a career change five years before I had the courage to quit. At that time, the faith of knowing that I am always taken care of was not apparent to me. Upon understanding that I was worthy of receiving support physically and spiritually, I was able to ask for it with total belief that it would appear.

The next selection entitled, "In This Moment," comes from my Reiki teachings. There are five main principles of Reiki: *Just for today; I will not anger; Just for today, I will not worry; Just for today, I will give thanks for my many blessings; Just for today, I will do my work honestly;* and *Just for today, I will honour every living thing.* These mantras are very powerful and constitute a positive model for everyone.

All of humanity following these spiritual directives every day would make a huge difference in our world. It is definitely something to aspire to and I do my best to live within these five laws.

In This Moment

Just for now, worry has no place in my heart.
I know it is useless to anticipate an outcome that seldom appears.
Just for now, I accept the flow of events, allowing the universe to
give me experiences that accelerate my growth at all levels.

Just for now, I refuse to let anger rule me.
Anger eats me up a piece at a time. It occupies
too much of myself and makes me weak.
Just for now, I release the effect of negative emotions
and respond only to those that elevate me.

Just for now, I work with integrity, acknowledging that what I
give out comes back to me. This is a bonus, not an expectation.
Just for now, I let go of all egotistical results, embracing
experiences that renew my spirit.

Just for now, I respect all living things, refusing to believe I am
more important than anyone or anything else. All life is precious.
Just for now, I accept being in harmony with all,
seeing myself as an integral part of the balance.

Just for now, I count my blessings, giving thanks for all I have.
I know my abundance is far more than I often acknowledge.
Just for now, I make the effort to see everything and everyone
around me for the amazing gifts they bring to my life.

Just for now, I surrender to the process of life, accepting that all my
experiences have led me to the perfection of who I am in this moment.

Present Moment Affirmations

1. My body, mind, and soul acknowledge this moment as the most important.
2. This moment brings my body, mind, and soul the lessons that take me closer to my definition of self.
3. This moment brings my body, mind, and soul the experience needed to complete the immediate lesson.
4. Only this moment can bring with it the understanding my body, mind, and soul crave.
5. My body, mind, and soul embrace this moment, realising that who I am right now is the gift I bring to the world.
6. My body, mind, and soul acknowledge that each moment is precious, but this one is invaluable.
7. Each moment I exist, I commit to the growth of my soul.
8. The experience of this moment brings lasting results.
9. My body, mind, and soul believe in the timelessness of this moment.
10. My body, mind, and soul surrender to the power this moment brings to my awareness.
11. My body, mind, and soul accept that time is an illusion that makes this moment all I have.
12. My body, mind, and soul understand that what I think, believe or do in this moment creates my reality.

> **Your questions are always answered. Acknowledging and acting on the response bring transformation.**

Have there been times in your life when you haven't understood the whys? Or possibly, have you understood them but had a difficult time accepting the answer? Losing a loved one to death is often an event that motivates the question why.

My first personal experience with death was when my mom passed on. It was a very emotional phase for me, especially since I was with her at the end of this cycle of her time.

The loss was not unexpected; we had been called in as a family during her remaining days. After being told that Mom didn't have much time left with us, my sisters and I took turns staying with her overnight at the care centre, where she had been living the last few months.

Perceptively knowing she was going to leave on my "shift," as I had witnessed every detail of it in my mind a few days before, I thought I would be prepared, and initially, I was. However, my readiness did not go beyond the prerequisite beginning stages.

When it happened exactly as I had envisioned that early morning in June just before dawn, I was calm and handled the calls to family and the other duties bereavement entails proficiently, but was not as prepared for the poignant impact of the reality of her death.

Emotionally overwhelmed and after another restless night, I awoke one morning a few weeks later to a caress on my cheek and knew instinctively—and without a doubt—it was Mom.

She brought me a great gift that summer morning: it was the gift of understanding life in a new way. With her transition to the next stage, I began anew.

This spiritual communication has led me straight to the path which I am on now. Something had been missing in my interpretation of existence. And when she transferred, my question "Is this all there is?" was answered.

There is more, so much more . . .

It Is You

It is you I lost that fateful day
You left me to find my way alone.
It is you who found me to softly whisper
That you always will be near.
It is you I feel in the gentle breeze
That touches the leaves on the trees.
It is you I see in the rainbow of colours
That cascade in an arch through the sky.
It is you I hear on a summer morning
In the bird's song as they greet a new day.
It is you who touch me with a warm kiss
When the sun shyly peeks out from a cloud.
It is you who listen when I want
To talk quietly or need to shout it out.
It is you I will never forget
Because I love you—you live within my heart.

Grief Affirmations

1. I give my body, mind, and soul the time to grieve, realising it is part of the human experience.
2. Before I allow grief to overwhelm me, I remember that energy never dies.
3. The grief my body, mind, and soul feel now comes from a sense of loss in physical experience, which is created by the illusion of tangibles.
4. I recognise the grief I feel as real but realise that loss is a human perception.
5. My body and mind choose to grieve for myself, but my soul realises that my loved one and me are connected in universal love, which is always present.
6. My body, mind, and soul embrace the memory of my loved one and see them as an extension of all there is.
7. My soul knows that physical death is a choice, and only fear of the unknown keeps the body and mind from trusting in the cycle of endless energy.
8. I allow my body and mind to acknowledge what my soul understands—physical death is spiritual rebirth.
9. My body, mind, and soul accept the choice my loved one has made in returning to their spiritual home.
10. I allow my body, mind, and soul to acknowledge my grief while being reassured that everything is as it should be.
11. I surrender to universal knowledge and release grief when I have accepted what is.
12. I forgive myself for losing faith in my higher power and reunite my body, mind, and soul in empowering trust of the universal plan.

Your experiences lead you to acknowledgement of self.

Sometimes, life experiences can leave us feeling unworthy and undeserving. This can be a pattern inherited from generations back, as we may have watched our parents struggling with self-acceptance just as they have watched theirs. Once self-doubt becomes an established blueprint, it can be difficult to release these negative self-beliefs, even if, at some level, they are unjustifiable.

In my family, there have been generations of alcohol abuse. Even while knowing this to be a form of escapism from the reality of life and feeling unable to handle perceived hardships, once established, the physical aspect of the addiction is difficult to break unless the subconscious cause is rectified.

My parents were both raised with at least one harsh disciplining parent, who was doing their best to handle their own self-destructive patterns. My paternal grandfather was a physical disciplinarian, and my maternal grandmother was verbally abusive. These two styles of parenting led to the relaxed parenting approach of my parents, who were determined—my mother especially—that their children would not be raised the way they were. Even though my father was a functioning alcoholic and my mother an enabler of this lifestyle, they were very approachable and supportive of us, their four daughters. There was never any harsh physical or verbal discipline in our house.

Though having been raised in a gentle, non-threatening home, I was unpredictable and angry much of the time during my childhood and adolescence, and my behaviour was of great concern to my parents.

Embarrassed about my family life—the drinking and living in what I considered near-poverty conditions—I made excuses to be anywhere other than at home. The feelings of not belonging and being different from the rest of the family had been persistent for the majority of my life.

When I began to release generational patterns of unworthiness several years ago, I realised that the persecution I felt was all self-inflicted.

Being

There are no flaws
In this world of perfection.
Trust in the universe,
See the connection.
Lessons to learn,
Experiences to see,
Worry is gone,
I realise all I can be.

As I make the choice
To acknowledge my inimitability,
To tell my truth
Without feeling futility,
The fear's held back;
While conviction and faith
Tell me I belong—
And that I am safe.

Feelings of persecution
Leave my connection broken.
Avoidance of my reality
Leave words unspoken.
Acceptance of self
Is a gift beyond measure,
Leaving trepidation behind
I open this treasure.

In freeing myself
I take nothing for granted;
The seeds now blooming
Are the ones God planted.
Understanding dawns, as again
And again—I fall.
Revealing the greater truth—
Belief in self is the strongest of all.

Being Affirmations

1. I am doing all I need to do when I let myself be me.
2. I forgive my body, mind, and soul for believing that doing is greater than being.
3. When I believe in myself, I am at my greatest strength.
4. I am continually amazed by my ability to pull myself up from fear into love.
5. Allowing myself to just be helps me to recognise who I am.
6. My body, mind, and soul connection to spirit is stronger every day.
7. I recognise that when I love myself for who I am, love is transmitted to those around me.
8. My body, mind, and soul are empowered by my belief in myself.
9. My body, mind, and soul accept loving myself for who I am.
10. My body, mind, and soul make the commitment to acknowledge myself as perfection.
11. I give my body, mind, and soul the freedom to open the treasure that is me.
12. My body, mind, and soul peacefully accept this life and the lessons it brings with courage and love, knowing I am who I choose to be.

> **Recognising that you are surrounded by angels keeps you at peace and in your power**.

Peace Descending was written as an antidote to my life. It puts many of my experiences into perspective, knowing that each event came and went, some with lasting effects and others with momentary impact. Each incident I have now assessed as a learning, which has led me to be the person I am. I have since attained peace, realising that every experience is one that I have signed up for at some level, whether consciously or subconsciously. At a conscious level, I didn't want to be a victim of sexual abuse or a car accident. But when I was heading off my destined path, the universe gave me a reminder alert. Some prompts were minor and others major, but each one made me aware that something was amiss. Unfortunately, I didn't always learn the lesson the first time, so the next occurrence appeared at double strength.

The experiences of sexual abuse in my life are a case in point, as each time my emotional meter rose considerably. I believe these situations contributed to the unworthiness issues I had lived with for many years. The first incident occurred when I was about six years of age by someone I trusted. It just felt wrong, even though the awareness of what was happening was not entirely evident to me at that age.

Other incidents occurred when I was older, and by then, I was wiser about the act, but not about the logic of it. After each abusive act, I would sink deeper into being a victim before realising that if I didn't do something about the situation, it would keep on happening. Upon understanding that the issue of power was at the core of these happenings, I knew the only one who could stop the behaviours and their aftermath was me—by changing how I saw myself. I had to take my power back! After giving it away a little at a time, there were only scraps left for me!

Working through the issues took some time, but bit by bit, I restored my self-worth by modifying beliefs about myself and forgiving the teachers who taught me such a harsh lesson. I am not defending improper behaviour; I'm just saying that everyone we learn from is a teacher.

No longer willing to carry the poison of negative energy, I want to heal completely, which includes acknowledging accountability around my experiences.

Peace Descending

Screaming, crying, tiny fists flailing;
Emerging into an unknown world.
Peace descending, as angels surround me.

Climbing, falling, small limbs breaking;
Anticipating the thud as I hit the ground.
Peace descending, as angels surround me.

Paralysed, unmoving, frozen in place;
Immobilising fear holds me still.
Peace descending, as angels surround me.

Maturing, conflicted, identity stripped;
Feeling so unlike myself.
Peace descending, as angels surround me.

Worried, anxious, waiting;
Unable to see my future ahead.
Peace descending, as angels surround me.

Lacking, unworthy, inadequate;
Not enough money to pay.
Peace descending, as angels surround me.

Running, yelling, choking on sobs;
My body is mine—leave it alone!
Peace descending, as angels surround me.

Fearful, disconnected, not okay;
Embracing substitutes for love.
Peace descending, as angels surround me.

Braking, crashing, metal crushing;
Unwanted images arising.
Peace descending, as angels surround me.

Disbelieving, unyielding, unable to feel;
Grieving for love once thought real.
Peace descending, as angels surround me.

Sighing, staring, stalling;
Precious life ebbing away.
Peace descending, as angels surround me.

Fighting, losing, finally allowing;
Accepting the light I see before me.
Peace descending, as angels surround me.

Screaming, crying, tiny fists flailing;
Emerging into an unknown world.
Peace descending, as angels surround me.

Peace Affirmations

1. Being at peace puts me in my power.
2. Knowing that I am always taken care of allows me to step out of my comfort zone.
3. My body, mind, and soul practise peace every day of my life.
4. I forgive my body, mind, and soul for believing that peace eludes me.
5. My body, mind, and soul embrace the peaceful moments, accepting that everything is as it is supposed to be.
6. My body, mind, and soul allow peace into my life, knowing I am worthy of serenity.
7. I show gratitude for angelic and universal support, trusting it will always be there for me.
8. My body, mind, and soul recognise angelic and universal support, especially in moments of distress.
9. My body, mind, and soul choose to ask for heavenly guidance when I feel lost in the illusion of pain.
10. I give my body, mind, and soul permission to think peaceful thoughts.
11. My body, mind, and soul release negativity, which dis-empowers me, and embrace divine love and tranquillity.
12. My body, mind, and soul are free to take back any power I have given away any time I have focused on or experienced conflict. I embrace peace.

> # The more you accept your own uniqueness, the more you have to contribute.

Living in the country, I have the opportunity to observe many animals. I have always understood that each type of animal displays individual characteristics, but their metaphysical significance was far more than I had ever comprehended.

Birds are very prominent in my life, and I see them as winged messengers. Ravens, robins, chickadees, crows, and blue jays are very visible in the area of Alberta, Canada, in which I live. Another bird I see often is the grouse, or prairie chicken, as we call it. This bird is very prominent, especially in the fall. When horseback riding we often come across a family of them, with the mother trying her best to lure us away from her babies. Now, these birds are not particularly fast and do not fly very high. They are able to settle in low bushes, and we see many of them in our mountain ash trees each fall or whole families scuttling across the gravel road when they are on the move.

The message these unique birds bring to us is one of drumming, as they beat their wings very loudly and rapidly. They also indicate coming into your power, and you begin to do that when you leave behind expectations of others and accept and display your own individuality.

As a person who once came from a place of feeling alienation and isolation, the grouse is an apt totem for me. It has shown me that dancing to my own beat is a valuable asset, and that loving myself for who I am—not for anyone else's perception of who I should be—is a quality to aspire to.

I was once afraid to show others the true me, fearing that I would not be acceptable to them and would not be good enough. I now realise that we all have something to give, everyone is perfect, and individuality is one of the greatest gifts you can give yourself and others.

Magic Dance

I strive to be as the grouse
Dancing to its rhythm,
Following nothing but the innate ability
To make its own interpretation.
The music of the world
Not affecting its style,
It creates the will to make its own.
Not following nor leading;
Just crafting the dance it feels.
Hearing the drumming beat in its head,
It remains untouched by anything
But retaining its own individuality.
As it circles and whirls,
It produces the style that suits itself this moment;
Neither wondering nor caring
Who watches or judges the action.
Just forming a new ripple,
Writing a new song,
Not for fame or acceptance;
But to feel joy fill its heart.

Individuality Affirmations

1. I allow myself to be me in all situations.
2. Retaining my individuality is a way of honouring myself.
3. My body, mind, and soul accept that who I am is all I need to be.
4. My body, mind, and soul are empowered by the knowledge that in accepting myself unconditionally, I release all judgements, which have kept me from living my life limitlessly.
5. My body, mind, and soul embrace the knowledge that in honouring myself, I honour God.
6. I believe in myself and my abilities.
7. I realise there is not another person exactly like me, which makes me invaluable.
8. My body, mind, and soul trust in my perfection.
9. When I receive love into my body, mind, and soul, I acknowledge that I am loveable.
10. I am committed to loving myself.
11. In loving myself, I am able to extend love to others.
12. I forgive my body, mind, and soul for believing I honour others by giving them my power.

> **Embrace joy every moment it appears**
> **and learn to expect it in your life.**

Have you ever had those moments when everything seemed absolutely ideal? Have you ever felt there was nothing that can ever disturb the perfection of the moment? That feeling is joy!

Before realising that there was more to life than work, paying bills, and just generally putting in time, instances of bliss were rare for me. Now, I feel them several times a day in the most ordinary moments. Joy is a state of mind, and the more it is experienced, the more expectation is placed on it to show up. The once-infrequent occurrences of delight have become increasingly commonplace, and inner peace has become a precedent for my life. The more happiness I have found, the more it has come my way.

Releasing the limitations of your definition of joy will increase the abundance of contentment you receive. If joy to you mainly includes superficial events like getting a raise, that perfect job or meeting the right person, think about increasing the size of that box. Take time to relish those seemingly uneventful moments such as watching the rain fall, welcoming silence when you are finally alone after being surrounded by people all day, observing children at play or other seemingly innocuous everyday events.

Taking the opportunity to embrace these moments will enhance your intuition as well, as you will start to recognise the signs of mental well-being and positive reinforcement your body displays as it responds to certain events.

I know that I am doing what is in my best interest when that explosion of pure joy resonates within my body. This is an affirmation that confirms to me that what I am thinking or doing is exactly what is needed at that instant.

Decisions are much easier now as verification comes from my feelings rather than through questioning or logical deduction.

At one time, I didn't allow myself to feel because insecurity and low self-esteem prevented me from making any kind of decision, just in case I was wrong or other people didn't agree with me. Now, my reaffirmed belief is that there is no right or wrong, only experiences.

Joy

There is joy in feeling the earth
Beneath my bare feet.
There is joy in watching the budding trees
Burst into leaf.
There is joy in the warmth of the sun
Upon my face.
There is joy in the wind blowing,
The clouds matching its pace.

There is joy in hearing
A child's laugh.
There is joy in knowing
I'm on the right path.
A trail that leads me to
Love I embrace.
Joy shows me
I'm in the right place.

Joy Affirmations

1. I embrace joy every moment of my life.
2. Joy gives my body, mind, and soul the freedom to see beyond the limits of material wealth.
3. Joy transforms my definition of life.
4. I forgive my body, mind, and soul for all the times I refused to accept joy because I believed my wants and needs were not being met.
5. My body, mind, and soul are committed to seeing joy all around me.
6. My body, mind, and soul have learned to see joy in the simple things.
7. Joyful moments are abundant in my life.
8. When my body, mind, and soul receive joy, my response sends positive energy out to others.
9. My body, mind, and soul understand that joy is a choice.
10. I fill my life with joy, which permits my body, mind, and soul to release anger and resentment.
11. Every part of my being resonates with joy.
12. When joy is abundant, negativity is overruled.

> ## In accepting your own magnificence,
> ## you are recognising the beauty in others.

What is it that determines a person's attractiveness? Is it one feature or a combination of different features? When only appreciative of the societal interpretation of beauty, people deemed physically unattractive are often rejected.

Beauty, to me, has undergone a considerable makeover since I have been doing face and body readings. I now get to know people by seeing their spirit rather than forming an opinion about them by their physical looks as a whole. Giving psychosomatic readings gives me the opportunity to be completely non-judgemental as well as an entirely new comprehension of personal lives and journeys. The information I receive is completely consistent with the course that person is on; as whatever lessons, experiences, or choices the individual has made are written on their face and body. I now understand that people are doing the best they can with what knowledge is available to them, and every one of us is truly and spiritually beautiful. If only we could all believe it!

Sometimes, with so much focus being placed on outward attractiveness, we forget to take care of our inner selves, which is where true beauty resides. Making positive changes from the inside will show on the outside!

A student whom I have known for almost two years was thirty-four years old when I met him but looked at least fifty. He is now a Master Teacher in the advanced discipline of Karuna Reiki and looks ten years younger than his chronological age. All the inner work he has done has erased the outward effects of emotional trauma from his appearance.

Your face shows others your personality—your essence—and being content and accepting of who you are will foster gratitude of each feature on it.

As we age, our physical appearance begins to show off our life experiences. Each grey hair and wrinkle indicates a recorded occurrence in our existence. The true self can be hidden from us and others in different ways, but the face and body are unable to hide secrets. Our corporeal attributes reflect the knowledge and understanding gained as we learn from our experiences.

This is true for everyone; therefore, seeing that person at their core for the outstanding being they are brings their essence into proper perspective.

Each one of us is beautiful and worthy. We all belong.

Faces

I see faces, faces everywhere,
All around, I see stories to share.
Faces reflecting who you are
Some up-close; many from afar.
What I see, I do not judge.
Anything revealed is meant as a nudge
To accept the journey as the one you chose;
Why you picked one so hard, God only knows.
With what we know, we walk our path;
Treading carefully in the aftermath
Of stopping short from hitting a wall;
Looking to find peace and joy in it all.

Some eyes squint with judgement,
From negative messages sent,
Others open wide with wonder
Through emotional storms with thunder.
Your nose can show an egotistical side—
A very obvious statement of pride.
Or perhaps a holding back of whom you can be
A side of yourself you let no one see.
Your mouth can be turned down with disdain,
Until joy turns it back up again.
Your chin tells me how strong your defences are
Does it jut out or only extend so far?

Your hair, your jaws, ears, and all the rest,
Tell me how you are faring on your quest.
The information is not to condemn you,
Merely another point of view
Of this journey you're making
And the steps you are taking.
Giant leaps or slow and small,
You are responsible for them all.
And who you meet along the way
Are those who can truly say,
"I am in your life to help all I can,
Even if it is sometimes hard to understand."

So, ride the wave—that is the plan,
Give credit to your fellow man.
And in every face you meet,
If you see resignation or defeat;
Know the lesson written there,
Is a plight you, too, may share.
See yourself in all and know,
Everyone's lessons help them to grow.
Accept that inside we are all the same,
Wanting love and acceptance, not blame.
So really look in the faces you see,
Not for condemnation, but for possibility.

Appearance Affirmations

1. I love every detail of my face as it shows the world who I am, and who I am is beautiful.
2. I refuse to allow the outside world to dictate to me what is beautiful.
3. I accept every part of my body, mind, and soul, knowing it constitutes the perfection of me.
4. When I allow others to judge me, I am accepting that they are wiser than me in their knowledge of who I am. I know myself better than anyone.
5. My face and body carry every lesson I have learned within them, and as I have become empowered by those lessons, my soul's beauty shines through.
6. My body, mind, and soul recognise my beauty.
7. I expel all biased comments about my appearance from my body, mind, and soul by myself and others, which have resulted in feelings of powerlessness.
8. In accepting and loving my appearance, I regain my power.
9. When I choose to accept the appearance of others, I expand my consciousness from physical limitations to spiritual enlightenment.
10. My body, mind, and soul release any preconceived ideas of beauty.
11. My body, mind, and soul see the beauty in all.
12. My body, mind, and soul believe that true beauty lives in the heart.

> **Give yourself the gift of silence. It will last forever, and its value appreciates each time you use it.**

Being bombarded with sound much of the time often makes it difficult to really relax. Noise—traffic, music, machinery—seems to be surrounding us wherever we are that silence consequently seems atypical.

I know many people who have become so accustomed to having noise around them at all times that they feel uncomfortable without it. Some of them have started incorporating just a few minutes of quiet contemplation into their day, thereby increasing the amount of time spent silently as their comfort zone accepting the noiselessness expands.

Allocating a part of your day to embrace calmness can make a difference to your experience of life. The stillness lets you get in touch with your inner being, as you are able to relate directly to self without distractions.

If you have not considered meditation because it is too difficult to sit for long periods in one place, engage in an activity that surrounds you with similar feelings of peace that formal meditation gives. Walking in the woods, working in the garden or, my favourite, horseback riding at dusk when everything is settling down for the night, are some ideas that, for me, bring serenity and a feeling of total connection with mind, body, soul and the universe as a whole.

I find those quiet moments that rebalance and centre me. Especially after a period of being immersed in noisy pursuits or having been consistently in contact with a lot of people, quiet moments are just what are needed for spiritual restructuring. Just a few minutes of tranquillity help to erase any stress acquired during a hectic day.

Take the time to recognise those moments when you feel at one with the world and yourself and incorporate them into your life as often as possible.

You will begin to notice a difference in your mood, and the feeling of belonging and connection to all of life will strengthen. Know that you are deserving of harmony, and learn to listen in the silence. You may be amazed by what you would hear!

In the Silence

In the silence, I can hear
All that which strengthens me;
I take the time to listen close,
As my heart speaks.

In the silence, I can hear
All that which empowers me;
I take the time to listen close
To the words of spirit.

Unencumbered by the needless noise
Of sounds, which tend to negate
Thoughts and feelings, only available—
In the silence.

Silence Affirmations

1. My body, mind, and soul recognise that silence allows me to gain self-knowledge.
2. In silence, my body, mind, and soul are rejuvenated.
3. I give my body, mind, and soul permission to accept silence.
4. When my body, mind, and soul are silent, I understand God.
5. My body, mind, and soul release all fear around being in silence and embrace enlightenment.
6. My body, mind, and soul are empowered by what I hear in silence.
7. My body, mind, and soul are committed to surrendering to the strength of silence.
8. In accepting silence, I embrace peace.
9. I permit my body, mind, and soul to expand my awareness through silence.
10. My body, mind, and soul release illusionary limits when I choose silence.
11. When I am silent, I can hear my heart speak.
12. Silence allows me to hear what is important.

> # You are never broken, but hiding your identity can cause chipping a piece at a time.

I met my husband when I was sixteen and he was twenty-one. We married three years later, and our two children were born within the next three years. Moving from my parents' house to my husband's, I was still maintaining the same subordinate role. At that time, I felt as if being someone's daughter, wife, mother, and eventually, someone's grandmother, was all I ever was and ever could be. Once the realisation hit that I was creating my own unhappiness by replacing my true identity with long-held personal beliefs, I was able to move into my own individuality.

Thanks to an emotional release process called Deep Cellular Healing, reclaiming my "self" allowed me to fit into the aforementioned roles without feeling as if I had to desert myself to play them. During the process of self-healing, I discovered that people meet my expectations when they treat me according to how I value myself, as well as the knowledge that receiving respect from others is redundant when self-respect is non-existent.

However, as things were changing for me on the inside, my outer world was becoming affected, mainly my relationship with my husband. He met the transformations I was experiencing with energetic resistance, and as I was growing spiritually, my husband was becoming unsure of his long-held role. Not willing to abandon myself, I left him. Our separation was temporary, and coming to terms with each other as individuals within our relationship was easier with respect and understanding (for us and for each other). Along with the willingness to accept each other's uniqueness, our journey together has now melded into a progressive commitment.

Although now, I do not believe we are ever broken—we just become disconnected from our source; when this piece was written, the title "My Broken Self" seemed appropriate because that was my feeling at that time.

Enough is too much when what you are doing does not produce the desired results anymore.

How much of yourself are you willing to give up for someone else? Your feelings of worthiness are determined by your choices.

My Broken Self

My spirit hovers in that place
Between happiness and where I feel safe.
Accepting that things will not change;
Love is gone; apathy remains.
I am scared for you and me,
But I'm making a choice to be free.
I don't want to be smothered anymore;
I feel wedged in—facing a hard, unyielding door.
Trying to be the person you wanted me to be,
Somewhere, I lost me.
I thought letting go of you
Was the hardest thing I had to do
But now I see—
It was really finding me!

Relationship Affirmations

1. My body, mind, and soul recognise relationships that empower me.
2. My body, mind, and soul are energised by relationships that enhance my understanding of self.
3. I forgive my body, mind, and soul for believing that staying in an abusive relationship helps me.
4. My body, mind, and soul allow me to express who I am in all relationships.
5. My body, mind, and soul understand that I am worthy and deserving of having unconditional love in my relationships.
6. My body, mind, and soul are empowered by the knowledge that I deserve respect.
7. My body, mind, and soul eradicate all beliefs that diminish my sense of self.
8. My body, mind, and soul recognise me as an individual within a relationship.
9. My body, mind, and soul have learned that good relationships are loving and supportive.
10. I receive abundant love and support in my relationships.
11. My body, mind, and soul are open to finding an intimate relationship that will honour me as an individual.
12. My body, mind, and soul take back any power I may have given away in my relationships.

Releasing your soul is not an ending; it is the beginning.

"Freedom to Fly" is the first poem I wrote after beginning my journey to awareness. It describes the unlimited feeling of freedom I have experienced after being locked up within myself for so long.

Upon understanding that I had choices and was worthy and deserving of having my dreams realised, the early stages of belief in myself led me to see the vision and meaning of my life.

By connecting my body, mind, and soul into one, I became whole. Instead of feeling disjointed, I recognised my soul as being part of me rather than functioning as a neglected child. Paying attention to it brought it into action as it reunited with my body and mind.

That was just the beginning. The further I travelled in this spiritual direction, the more opportunities presented themselves in the form of people, books, and ideas.

I met people who were on parallel paths, came upon books to facilitate growth, and generated ideas for helping myself and others to expand our awareness.

It soon became my life's mission to assist other people who were ready to heal. As I am still learning and growing, I am acknowledging that the people who become my students are also my teachers, as is everyone who connects with me at any level on this journey.

My life's expansion began with a decision that resulted from the recognition that I was more than this body and wasn't using all of my potential but just a tiny part of it. The result of that resolution to find the imprisoned pieces of myself has led to peace and liberty from self-imposed restraints.

My wish for you is that you also embrace your soul and find the freedom to fly, dream, and live in the way we are all meant to—with passion, purpose, and unbridled enthusiasm for life.

Freedom to Fly

Soar high on the wings of an eagle;
Dive to the depths of the sea;
My vision goes beyond the realms of time,
As I'm inspired by dreams in me.

I never held such freedom to fly;
Chains of traditional thought had enslaved me.
Now a key has turned the lock and released my heart;
My imprisoned dreams given licence to be free.

Fragile dreams buried as hope or disguised as a wish
I need not chase again, for now held open in my hand,
They are ready for the gentle, awakening kiss
Of life.

Freedom Affirmations

1. My body, mind, and soul have learned that there are no limits where there is freedom.
2. In freeing myself, my body, mind, and soul recognise unlimited resources within me.
3. My body, mind, and soul are happy to be free.
4. My body, mind, and soul accept freedom as my birthright.
5. Freedom allows me to expand my knowledge and understanding.
6. My body, mind, and soul believe in the freedom to fly.
7. My body, mind, and soul transcend the limiting beliefs I formerly held.
8. My body, mind, and soul move forward, freeing myself from thoughts and beliefs that have paralysed me with fear.
9. My body, mind, and soul embrace new paradigms that bring new knowledge.
10. I am free to create my life.
11. In the places of my body, mind, and soul where I once felt encumbered by limits, I now acknowledge the freedom of choice.
12. I forgive myself for the restrictions I have placed upon my body, mind, and soul.

A life of gratitude is a blessing in itself.

Gratitude is one of the single most important elements that can foster change in all areas of your life. All the things you are grateful for today bring more of those to be grateful for tomorrow.

Attainment has become a pastime for many—money, a new house, a new car, and all the illusions of success—that simple things are becoming more insignificant. Working more hours to make more money to buy more things now constitutes a majority of lifestyles in our modern world.

I, too, once missed seeing many of the significant elements surrounding me each day. After realigning my focus to include my soul's preferences pertaining to abundance rather than always alluding to what my body and mind wanted, I now find hundreds of things to be grateful for daily. In simple enjoyments—like finding lost items, a friend calling, my horses coming in from the pasture to meet me halfway, the sun shining after days of rain or snow—are where I find pleasure. Expressing gratitude for what is around me brings additional things for me to appreciate.

People who have what you think you want are not luckier than you are; they simply have the vibration that brings whatever they request to them. They recognise that there is always enough for everyone, and that nobody has to go without. They are willing to share because they know there is always more for everybody, and they see nothing as ever depleted because too many already have it.

This solid belief in abundance and in your own worth allows you to receive what you want. This profusion is not just for some; it is available to all.

Focus on what you want in your life. Say "Thank you" for the little joys as well as the bigger ones. Allow yourself to receive by centring your attention on what you already have, and notice the difference this awareness brings into all areas of your being. Your body, mind, and soul will rejoice.

Each Day's Promise

As each new day begins, I am filled with wonder
That the unconsciousness of the night brings forth
Such beauty in the morning light.
The sun streams through my window, illuminating beams of dust.
And when I see the suggestion of green on the tops of the trees
Through the natural blue of the sky,
I feel a pull to get up and greet the awakening of a new day.

Each day holds such promise of accomplishment.
Answers to my questions unveil as the day moves forward,
Before it slowly draws into night again.
Each day holds familiarity as well as the anticipation of newness.
No day is ever quite the same as the last,
Though it may seem so around the edges.
Only I know the difference of my thoughts yesterday, from today.

As each new day brings a new question,
A new answer,
A new excitement to it,
I realise the treasure of abundance I have:
A universe ready and willing to give all that is asked of it.
Asking and receiving is for everyone.
Those who realise it are no more deserving than anyone else is—
They have just come to believe in the power of this great
universe to give.
The gratitude is genuine.

Gratitude Affirmations

1. My body, mind, and soul recognise the importance of all blessings in my life.
2. My body, mind, and soul appreciate the beauty that surrounds me.
3. My body, mind, and soul trust in the infinite abundance of the universe.
4. I awake each morning trusting that today is a miraculous day.
5. I go to sleep each night with gratitude in my body, mind, and soul for the blessings of the day.
6. My body, mind, and soul allow me to enjoy the great universal gift of life.
7. My body, mind, and soul realise I can have whatever I desire.
8. My body, mind, and soul surrender to the knowledge that I am worthy and deserving of having all my wishes realised.
9. I give my body, mind, and soul permission to accept the well-deserved blessings offered to me every day.
10. My body, mind, and soul are empowered to understand that I am worthy of unconditional love.
11. Each day, I empower my body, mind, and soul to the realisation that I create positive intention through my thoughts.
12. My body, mind, and soul are ready to receive infinite universal blessings.

> **In the darkness glows a light; it begins as a sliver, but soon, its brilliance will dazzle you.**

Driving up a hill in my car, I am unable to see beyond the crest of the hill; but I know once I reach the top, there will be a path on the other side to safely bring me to my destination.

This analogy applies to life as well. There are lessons that may seem tough, some harder than others, but eventually we do descend to the learning side of that experience. The seemingly difficult times may appear to be all-consuming when things are not going as smoothly as we would like. Although unable to see what is on the other side, knowing that light will materialise and lift us out of the darkness is a comforting thought. When the light appears, it will emerge even brighter then we remember it being initially.

It is at the darkest point just prior to the appearance of the sliver of light that we make a vibrational shift preceding a period of growth when new knowledge is available to us. This experience brings with it a fresh understanding as well as a different perspective around the issue we have just explored and the resulting accomplishment of overcoming the obstacle we had thought as insurmountable at the beginning.

Though our perception of these lessons may be overstated, knowing that light always follows darkness can help bring about manageability of the learning stage.

Our strength and resilience are remarkable, and the subconscious mind realises that our capabilities are greater than our conscious mind often acknowledges.

"This too shall pass" is a favourite mantra of mine during those times when fear appears to defeat love. But there is one thing I do know without a doubt: love always prevails in the end.

Time of Darkness

The storm of life is as the seasons—
Here for a time, then disappearing;
Though not all at once
But slowly reducing its intensity,
Until only traces remain:
And then—nothing.

The light will shine again
In the time of darkness.
I smile through my tears,
As love eases the pain.

Although now I feel as if
The warmth of light is gone
And things will never be the same;
The ache slowly eases,
Until only traces remain:
And then—nothing.

The light will shine again
In the time of darkness.
I smile through my tears,
As love eases the pain.

Life is leaving me far behind
And I see the grief of those
Who have loved me.
I cling and slowly let go,
Until only traces remain:
And then—nothing.

The light will shine again
In the time of darkness.
I smile through my tears,
As love eases the pain.

Universal Love Affirmations

1. My body, mind, and soul acknowledge the love of the universe as everlasting.
2. The power of universal love fills my entire being with joy.
3. My body, mind, and soul realise my worthiness in receiving universal, unconditional love.
4. My body, mind, and soul recognise me as being an essential part of the universal plan.
5. In accepting myself, I allow my body, mind, and soul to gain the freedom to trust in the light that always appears.
6. I give my body, mind, and soul the freedom to receive support at all levels.
7. I synergise my body, mind, and soul to the energy of unconditional love and support of the universe.
8. My body, mind, and soul remember to look for the sliver of light that always appears in times of darkness.
9. My body, mind, and soul understand that only love is real; everything else is illusion.
10. My body, mind, and soul embrace the knowledge that love eases the pain.
11. I forgive my body, mind, and soul for the times I have slipped into darkness and have forgotten to look for the light.
12. My body, mind, and soul release the energy that has kept me from remembering my perfection as I permit myself to open up to love.

> **Love is always free to give, and unconditional love costs nothing to receive.**

If I asked one hundred people what their definition of love was, I would probably get one hundred different answers. The word "love" seems to resonate with individual experience and perception. There is romantic love, parental love, or love for a friend, sibling, or relative. Used in this context, love is a noun, which is a word that describes a place, person, or thing. Saying "I love you" to someone is a verbal expression, which according to the Merriam-Webster dictionary is "a word that combines the characteristics of a verb (action word) with those of a noun or adjective."

Unconditional love is given and received without the expectation for something in return. If it becomes dependent on what is given back to you, it may still be love you feel but with extenuating circumstances, which is not love in its highest form. The action of absolute love, whether for oneself or another, requires the giver to be completely free of judgement and discrimination.

Striving to give love without hesitation is still a challenge to me at times, but then, I have yet to release all judgement around myself. Loving myself wholly and without reservation would permit me to send love out the same way. Each conscious step leads me closer to my goal of loving myself and others totally.

I am now able to identify and catch myself most times when I'm not living up to my full potential in loving without censure. Being on the human learning curve and acknowledging that there are still times when the results don't always meet my resolutions, I have realised that giving myself permission to forgive myself is essential to promoting all levels of growth.

To answer my own questions in the following poem, I would have to say, "No, love is not always easy for me to give or simple to receive, but being aware of my limitations allows my acknowledgement of them."

With awareness, you can take action. Without it, the dormant knowledge imprisons you with inertness.

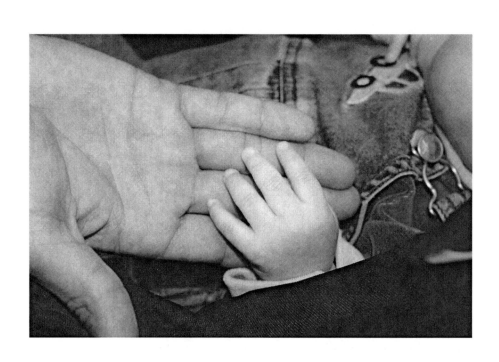

Love in Action

When I hear you say "love,"
It sounds like a place or a thing,
Love is not something to possess.
It is for you to give.

With love being your essence,
The giving of it is the giving of you.
This eternally active cycle
Begins in the stirrings of your own heart.

To give is to receive.
And in accepting love, you
Acknowledge your own worthiness,
Valuing yourself in your choice.

It is easy to say you love.
Is it as easy to give?
Is it as simple to receive?
The answer begins with you.

When I hear you say "love,"
It sounds like a place or a thing,
Love is not something to possess.
It is for you to give.

Love Affirmations

1. The love I show to myself extends out to others.
2. Loving and accepting myself are the first steps to showing unconditional love to others.
3. I allow my body, mind, and soul the freedom to love myself unconditionally.
4. As my soul evolves, the ability to love myself becomes easier.
5. I embrace the love that is shown to me by others, with the knowledge that receiving love is a step towards loving myself unconditionally.
6. My body, mind, and soul acknowledge my worthiness when I receive the love extended to me by others with grace and ease.
7. My body, mind, and soul realise that the more I love myself, the easier it becomes to love others.
8. I forgive my body, mind, and soul for believing that I need to receive anything in return when I show love to others.
9. My body, mind, and soul understand the ability to love coming from the action of the heart.
10. In the places of my body, mind, and soul where I have withheld love from myself and others, I now release it to be accepted by all who want it.
11. I value myself and others by accepting love from all who extend it.
12. I believe my body, mind, and soul deserve to be loved unconditionally.

> **Allow the ordinary to refresh you—not to avoid change but to recall your humanness.**

Sometimes, being caught up in the seriousness of life and all it entails makes us forget the common things that are an important part of our existence. Often, we misplace our priorities and take everyday things for granted, letting what we assume to be more important activities take precedence over our usual daily practises.

It is the regular events that help us refresh when we become too stressed or caught up in the busyness of life. Just knowing that some things stay the same day after day brings a certain calmness. This routine can help put things into perspective.

How many of us can't wait to get back to the ordinary after a long holiday or an illness? We just know our usual place in the world is there waiting for us.

I am not saying we should embrace the mundane and avoid change; it's quite the contrary. Change is essential to life, and it is to be accepted and honoured to accelerate our growth. But there are times when just visiting the daily sameness can revitalise us.

Focusing on simple, standard, everyday programming helps keep us grounded and aware of the importance of agenda in the human experience. Many lessons have been created and accomplished in and around the revolving patterns of our lives.

Embracing the ordinary and looking at it from a different angle other than the same old viewpoint can change the experience from one of humdrum and boredom to one of excitement. Knowing that being able to create a new reality from an old paradigm gives us the opportunity to expand our limits and move away from our comfort zone.

Coming back to the ordinary from time to time also enables us to recognise how far we have come and how much more we intend to create.

Ordinary Things

Talk to me of ordinary things.
What you did today?
At work—how did it go?
Whom did you see?
Talk to me of ordinary things
That which each and every day brings.

When you speak of ordinary things,
All that pressures me
Stops in its tracks—ceasing in its movement;
Becoming less important.
Talk to me of ordinary things
That which each and every day brings.

All this talk of ordinary things
Brings me peace,
Knowing day to day—the sameness
Can be counted on.
Talk to me of ordinary things
That which each and every day brings.

Grounding Affirmations

1. I am reminded of my humanness when I give the ordinary things attention.
2. My body, mind, and soul are grounded each time I embrace ordinary patterns in my life.
3. I open my body, mind, and soul to the understanding that peace comes in many forms.
4. I release stress in my body, mind, and soul when I embrace the ordinary.
5. I forgive my body, mind, and soul for believing that routine is futile.
6. My body, mind, and soul are relaxed and at peace when I appreciate daily events.
7. The richness of my life is enhanced when I embrace the simple things.
8. Opening up to new perspectives within daily routines allows my body, mind, and soul to value my earthly existence.
9. My body, mind, and soul love to evolve simply and calmly.
10. Centring my attention on the little things allows my body, mind, and soul to appreciate a new perspective.
11. I am reminded of my experiences as a spiritual being in human form when I welcome routine.
12. My body, mind, and soul appreciate the lessons I learn from everyday experiences.

> ## Accepting that I am responsible for my choices gives me the power to transform them.

At one time, I believed I didn't have choices in my life, but since releasing that belief, I now know that I have chosen my experiences whether I interpret their results as negative or positive.

When I chose to abuse my body with alcohol and cigarettes as a teenager and young adult, I blamed my family situation. After all, wasn't it a learned behaviour? As long as I believed it was someone else's fault, nothing was going to change.

Upon accepting responsibility for the decisions I had made, guilt became my belief of choice for a time before I realised that holding on to another negative emotion was just as destructive to my body as the substances I fed it. I was able to move forward by releasing guilt and seeing that particular time in my life as an experience without having to justify or label it.

Our choices relate to the beliefs we have about ourselves. If we believe we are loveable, we will bring people and situations into our life that support that concept. The opposite is also true. By carrying the belief that we have no control over our life, we will encounter people and situations that sustain that conviction as well.

Taking responsibility for what we have created becomes an important part of changing what we deem to be unacceptable and superfluous. It is exciting to know that whatever we have produced is reversible: if we feel it no longer represents our essence, we can choose to let it go. Energy modalities are available and are designed to help with releasing undesirable emotional baggage no longer wanted in your life.

The one I use and teach is Deep Cellular Healing. It is simplistic in method and very effective. Without having to rehash old experiences, it simply allows you to identify the core situation or emotion; let that old negative energy go and replace it with positive intent. The difference it has made in my life is huge!

I Am

I face today with gratitude:
For all that I have;
For all that I am;
For all I will be.

I end today with thanks:
For all that I have been given;
For all that I have received;
For all I have become.

I will do this again tomorrow
When it becomes today;
I will do this every day so
At the end of this life
I can say:
"I am who I have chosen to be!"

Choices Affirmations

1. I forgive my body, mind, and soul for believing I have to hold on to guilt around the choices I have made.
2. My body, mind, and soul recognise that the choices I have made culminate in my experiences, and I release labels or judgement around the results of those experiences.
3. My body, mind, and soul recognise the experiences I have had as a platform for the wisdom I have acquired.
4. My body, mind, and soul see beyond my choices to the underlying lesson.
5. In releasing judgement around my experiences, I acquire knowledge beyond the superficial.
6. My body, mind, and soul accept responsibility for the choices I have made.
7. My body, mind, and soul are empowered by my choices.
8. My body, mind, and soul are grateful for my experiences.
9. My belief in myself overcomes the fear of making the wrong decision.
10. In understanding my experiences, I eradicate any negative beliefs I have taken on as a result of my choices.
11. My body, mind, and soul are committed to making choices that further my growth on all levels.
12. My body, mind, and soul release any fear that prohibits me from making decisions that enhance my development at all levels.

**Learn to look beyond the illusion,
and the pieces will fit together perfectly.**

Life is so full of opposites that overwhelming confusion often inhibits our sense of direction. You cannot become independent by always relying on someone else just as you cannot transform your life if you are unwilling to make any changes.

Desiring positive results, we often endeavour to receive them by focusing on the opposite, which is the negative. We attempt to promote peace by declaring war, and use force in place of understanding and love. Expecting to receive love by sending out hate or to produce joy when the emphasis is on sorrow is a mania of paradoxical thinking.

Realising this at some level, theory is not always put into practice as we tend to hold on to what is known, being stifled by limitations placed upon us by ourselves. Producing some energetic movement by effort creates more of what we are attempting to alleviate, as an immediate resolution beyond what has already been attempted is not always impending. So by wanting some kind of result, the same overused, imperfect answer reintroduces itself to reproduce an unsatisfactory outcome.

The correct solution does not have to be forced—it just fits. It feels right and provides the result you are wanting without creating detrimental residue.

I remember searching for something as a young adolescent and into my adult years. I didn't know what it was but knew I was missing a piece somewhere. I would attend various churches, go to a few services at each one, and then drop out. Nothing felt right to me. After being introduced to spirituality in the form I now embrace, my search was over. From the beginning, it felt like I was home. Your reality may differ from mine, but I know this to be my truth.

The appropriate solution always repairs the fundamental problem. If the desired end result is delayed or non-existent, the answer lies somewhere else. Doing the same thing repeatedly without an anticipated outcome does not only make no sense, it is a total waste of energetic fortitude.

Illusionary Conflict

Strong, yet gentle,
Graceful, but powerful;
Nothing's more conflicted
Than our illusionary life.

Seeing but without understanding,
Wanting abundance, but living in lack;
Desiring love, we promote hate.
Ah, our illusionary life.

We strive for individuality, but long to belong,
We want peace, but make war;
Embracing our earth and harming it too.
Oh, our illusionary life.

We strive to be positive, but cling to the negative.
We speak of God as love, but reject him,
Creating fear where we once held faith.
Interesting—our illusionary life.

We ask forgiveness, but seek revenge,
Wanting change, but refusing it;
Searching for health, but invading our body,
Nothing like our illusionary life.

We attempt to laugh, but cry for joy,
Wanting to be loved, but being judgemental;
So loving, yet so capable of being hurtful;
Yet we embrace our illusionary life.

Strong, yet gentle,
Graceful, but powerful;
Nothing's more conflicted
Than our illusionary life.

Transformation Affirmations

1. My body, mind, and soul release the limitations I have created that impair my desired results.
2. My body, mind, and soul liberate the fear that has kept me at a standstill until this moment.
3. I enable my body, mind, and soul to move forward from limiting fear.
4. In order to honour my soul's purpose, my mind and body transcend limitations and create new possibilities.
5. My body, mind, and soul are open to courage, which enhances my ability to create new solutions.
6. I forgive my body, mind, and soul for holding on to the belief of self-sabotage I have been carrying.
7. My body, mind, and soul realise unlimited possibilities for change.
8. My body, mind, and soul understand how to produce desired results.
9. My body, mind, and soul have the ability to change the direction of my life for the better.
10. I give my body, mind, and soul the wisdom to discriminate between an illusionary solution and one that holds a viable resolution.
11. My body, mind, and soul send out love and understanding to countries, people, and animals in distress.
12. My body, mind, and soul join with others as one to create a circle of light, which holds the earth and its inhabitants in a cycle of love.

> ## Even the smallest creature deserves
> ## to be honoured for its purpose.

All life is precious and has meaning. Even though we may sometimes wonder what the purpose of some life forms is, we can be sure that each living thing is meant to be.

Each creature has a lesson for us; we only need to watch, listen, and learn. I work spiritually with insects, birds, and animals of all kinds and physically with a few domestic ones. The power of their presence is amazing, and every one of them has a unique metaphysical meaning. No living thing can be discounted, as the smallest insect often carries the strongest message.

Honouring the energy of every creature brings them closer, encourages more frequent contact, and therefore, more interchanges between us. Even if you are not sure what communication they bring, just taking the time to be present and appreciative while they are within your sight will strengthen the bond that connects all life. Of course, always keep in mind that wild animals are easily frightened, so allow them their space.

Here in the country, I can look outside just about any given day and see animals in their natural setting. Deer, coyotes, and even moose reside in our yard at various times of the year. They come for a visit for a few days and then move on. I have seen horses lying just a short distance away from resting coyotes, and deer often sharing horses' feed. A few years ago, when I left for work on a dark winter morning, a moose was standing just a few feet from my car. Occasionally a bear will wander down our road, just passing through.

Even the neighbour's domestic animals have come to visit. We have had dogs, horses, a donkey, and even a pig at one time or another.

Animals generally know their boundaries, and if they aren't honouring them, look at yourself. It may be a message on how you are handling your own borders.

Symbolic Synergy

The trees sway in the calm, gentle breeze,
Fluffy clouds drift by, a movement one barely sees.
As magpies dip and dive to the ground
Ravens fly overhead, making their cawing sound.

The squirrels pause once or twice
Then scamper on with their busy lives.
Robins hop about on the ground,
Searching for worms in every dirt mound.

Tiny spiders, webs they form;
An intricate design is the norm.
Lives are spent creating beauty,
For them—it's a sense of duty.

Honeybees around flowers swarm
To sip the nectar while it is warm.
Flies and mosquitoes add to the buzz;
Is it solely to annoy us?

All of nature at its best;
Could this possibly be a test
To help us see and reflect
On all of life and how we interconnect?

Communication Affirmations

1. I allow communication with all in my mind, body, and soul.
2. My mind, body, and soul appreciate every form of life.
3. My mind, body, and soul choose to receive information designed for my highest good.
4. In the places of my mind, body, and soul where I have declined messages out of fear, I now accept to receive them out of love.
5. I give my body, mind, and soul the ability to act on the communications I receive.
6. My mind, body, and soul acknowledge and appreciate the messages I receive each day.
7. My mind, body, and soul embrace universal communications.
8. I empower my mind, body, and soul to receive universal communication.
9. My body, mind, and soul are free to communicate at all levels.
10. My body, mind, and soul are attuned to universal wisdom.
11. Communicating my thoughts and ideas is easy for me.
12. My body, mind, and soul love, understand, and value the earth and all of its inhabitants.

> **Our connection with each other and our universe is limitless and transcends time.**

Accepting that we are all one puts an entirely different meaning on the concept of you and me. If you believe, as I do, that we all started from the same particle of matter, then each of us carries a small part of the other, establishing another perspective on the meaning of unity. Being linked to one another this way means that we are influenced by the experiences, attitudes, and beliefs of others.

This connection is so close that even if I think a negative thought about another person, they can take that thought into their subconscious. Depending on how self-empowered they are, the recipient of my judgement will either reject my viewpoint or absorb it to add another scar to their already-overwhelmed self-esteem.

Now, by putting that negative impression out there, I have created a situation not only for my victim but for myself as well because I am also going to be affected by that energy. Discharging negative impressions each day creates an overwhelming impact on our already-stressed world.

Healing individually by letting go of emotions that influence us to lash out and hurt others to feel better about ourselves will bring about a multi-curative effect, as everyone will benefit. Each of us making the effort to come to terms with our own feelings of powerlessness by learning to love ourselves can make a difference in everyone.

When I look back, though I grew up in a family that had a lot going for it, I did not accept myself, so I blamed them for my own sense of rejection. Feeling unlike them, I imposed my own attitude of not fitting in on both my original and present families.

It took me a while to discover the light within myself, and when I did, I was able to realise it in them. This light is in all. Find the radiance inside yourself and you will have no difficulty seeing it in others.

Oneness

The energy flows from my soul to yours,
And from your soul to mine;
Searching, seeking out those places
Where light has hidden;
Reaching far beyond the perimeters
Of all we can see.
Our knowledge and understanding
Lead to acceptance
Of what we have always known
But throughout time have forgotten:
We are connected.

Connection Affirmations

1. Knowing we are all one, my body, mind, and soul accept seeing the light in others.
2. My body, mind, and soul trust in the universal connection of oneness.
3. I see myself as an integral part of the universal consciousness.
4. My body, mind, and soul employ the belief that my contribution to universal consciousness is valuable.
5. My body, mind, and soul are empowered to release negative judgements of others as I now realise that my thoughts affect all.
6. My body, mind, and soul embrace others in an understanding that reaches farther than I can see.
7. My body, mind, and soul commit to accepting and embracing all, knowing that the light within me is in everyone.
8. My body, mind, and soul understand that accepting every part of me is the groundwork to reaching out to others.
9. My body, mind, and soul acknowledge that the collective consciousness, when utilised in a positive manner, exemplifies love and compassion for all. I therefore wholeheartedly embrace it.
10. Each day, I take the time to send out loving thoughts.
11. My body, mind, and soul realise that my manifesting skills are supreme and I have the power to change the world with my thoughts.
12. I believe in my ability to make the world a better place.

> **Limitless possibilities exist. You just have to open the door, remove the walls, and raise the ceiling.**

Being so truly awed at the learning that has taken place in my life and how far I have been propelled forward since beginning this journey of awakening, I often go deep inside my soul to see what else will develop. That is where the next selection called "What if?" came from.

Openings are all around me, and the self-imposed limits that once were so easy for me to confine myself in are completely gone. There are no walls where I now exist. Where difficulties once resided, grace and ease now reign.

The complicated situations I found myself in were of my own making, as I was the one who made my life hard by the decisions and choices that prompted the lessons that appeared. My fear-based results were achieved from a foundation of anxiety-inspired thinking.

Having now opened up to all possibilities without fear make my life limitless. Two of my favourite mantras are "It is what it is" and "I am always amazed." What can be better than being totally open to amazement?

By trying to control things, we are opting to suppress surprise. Surprises come in the form of the unexpected; so in eliminating them, existence becomes no more than accepting the usual circumstances and expecting the limits we have placed on it.

Reducing the unusual within our lives may feel like a safe choice, but it also brings with it a lack. By living only with what we know and within the boundaries of our reality, we are not allowing imagination and creativity to hold a place in our subsistence. These two elements combined with infinite possibility allow us to open up to conjecture, to believe in the mystery of life, and live joyfully.

I doubt my life lessons are completely over, but the tools I have acquired on my journey have thus far enabled me to look at things differently. From this new perspective and belief in my ability, I welcome the transformation that always follows the teaching.

What if?

As I cling to the last threads of recognition
Before drifting off to sleep,
My mind suddenly grabs awareness
Once again, as a thought assails me;
What if it is not reality I'm leaving
As I sleep—but a dream?
Suppose reality begins the moment
Unconsciousness takes over from the day;
Are our thoughts, perceptions, and ideas
Only an illusion of actuality?
And are our dreams and unconscious
Thoughts our only truth?
Do I keep my real self hidden among
The mysteries of the night and allow
The illusion of self to appear
Within the light of day?
Do I take the remembrances of my
Day life into my sleep to awaken
Into veracity and review bits and pieces
As to how they fit into that world?
These things I wonder as daylight streams around me.
Then, when night falls again, I question
What if?

Letting Go Affirmations

1. My body, mind, and soul acknowledge the possibility that letting surprises into my life allows me to expand my limits.
2. My body, mind, and soul let go of preconceived beliefs that controlling outcomes keeps me from encountering difficulty in my life.
3. My body, mind, and soul trust in the process of life and infuse me with the knowledge that I am safe.
4. My body, mind, and soul are accustomed to allowing life to surprise me.
5. My body, mind, and soul welcome amazement into my life.
6. My body, mind, and soul release the preoccupation of always having to know the outcome before it appears.
7. My body, mind, and soul believe in miracles.
8. My body, mind, and soul realise the importance of following my dreams.
9. My body, mind, and soul understand the freedom that letting go of fear creates.
10. My body, mind, and soul embrace imagination and creativity.
11. I trust my body, mind, and soul to release limits that hold me back from accomplishment.
12. My body, mind, and soul release beliefs around lack and receive abundance.

The impression of your energy is forever.

We are an unending cycle of energy, and although we may show up in different containers each time, our soul never dies.

I believe that the feeling of association we have with certain people is the connective energy from a life lived before meant to help us realise that there is something greater than most of us can physically see, hear, or touch.

Our energy remains behind once we leave our earthly existence and transfers to a higher plane. The essence and wisdom imparted to those we connect with while we were here resound long after we have gone on.

What I remember most about my dad is his philosophy of life. Having been a tank driver in World War 2, he had lived through horrific happenings but was able to use those incidents to create an understanding that may be far beyond the knowledge of those who hadn't been involved in the conflict. He refused to speak of the war unless he was drunk, but I believe his outlook and point of view came about because of those experiences. His characteristic approach was one of "live and let live," and he took every event in his life in stride. He never refused to help anyone in difficulty. I remember having several different, troubled teenagers or young adults living in our home at various times during my childhood and teenage years. That legacy lives on and is very apparent in both of my children, who are now adults themselves.

Leaving an impact on everyone we come in contact with and what we do with these relationships determine the outcome of our imprint. It is up to us to decide how we want to be remembered in each reintegration.

We are all energy, and energy never dies, so renewing our spirit time after time and accessing a new body allow us to continue on to attain higher spiritual enlightenment.

How can someone as precious as you only have one time around?

Unending Cycle

The circle of life does not end with death,
It only begins anew.
Do not fear that very last breath,
You will forever be you!

The heart stops beating,
The body breaks down.
At this—the last meeting,
The soul homeward bound.

Soul is released.
Limits left behind,
Full potential unleashed
As earthly ties cease to bind.

We create the illusion of reality
As within this shell we subside.
We see this life as mortality
Though there's a bigger story inside.

Life we know is a gift:
And when we choose to leave;
Our lessons learned, we make the shift;
Our loved ones left to grieve.

Once gone, we comprehend
How we lived, as fair or grand;
But usually not till then
Do we completely understand.

Our life is exactly as we choose;
And whatever we create:
Maybe pay our karmic dues—
Or have cause to celebrate,

It is ours to give our best,
We obtain what we demand.
So, at the end, we can attest,
My life was at my command!

Life Choices Affirmations

1. My body, mind, and soul recognise the power within me to make choices that enhance my life.
2. My body, mind, and soul claim the power to make appropriate choices.
3. In the places of my body, mind, and soul where I have felt defenceless, I now embrace choice.
4. My body, mind, and soul understand that I am who I am because of my choices.
5. My body, mind, and soul now commit to making choices, which amplify my light within and extinguish those which no longer serve me.
6. I forgive my body, mind, and soul for past choices, which do not define my true essence.
7. My body, mind, and soul realise the importance of making appropriate choices that enhance my life.
8. The definition of who I am is evident in the superior choices I make.
9. In the past, I may have acted the part of a victim, believing I was not responsible for my life. My body, mind, and soul now release that belief and accept responsibility for who I am.
10. Every life I choose allows me to access higher vibrations of energy, which project me closer to my goal of enlightenment.
11. My body, mind, and soul are no longer dependent on the beliefs of others.
12. My body, mind, and soul see physical death as a spiritual rebirth, which eradicates any fear of dying I have.

> **The presence of a higher power in your life,
> no matter what name you give it, is a reminder of
> your integral connection and contribution to life.**

The idea of God has many interpretations. Although the energy of a higher power goes by many names, that unconditional, loving presence is anywhere you choose to look.

When all appears well in your life, your association with God is abundant, fulfilling, and rewarding. It seems easier to find "God" when all is right in your world as your vibration is high, showing your connection to universal power.

Being in a low state of vibration, this source is harder to recognise because you have disconnected from it. The thing is, those low points are when we seem to need that caring, peaceful energy the most. These moments of distress give us the opportunity to reconnect.

When I was in a negative space, it was easier for me to renounce than accept God's presence. Choosing to remain a victim was a way of proving to myself (and others) that I was justified in my actions. In my suffering, I reserved the right to hold on to whatever issue was bothering me. The longer I lingered in retaining that "poor me" status, the harder it was to bring myself out of it. So that low energy state stuck with me for long periods.

Surrendering to the knowledge of a higher power in my life afforded me the opportunity to grow and change. By admitting to and accepting the presence of God, I was unable to remain in that lower state, as initiating the bond with Spirit retrieved and revitalised my vibrational frequency.

Recognising that God is everywhere no matter how you are feeling at that time makes it almost impossible to remain disconnected. Identifying one thing that reminds you of your true essence re-establishes the connection and resumes your vital relationship with all of life.

Everywhere

Today I met God
And God was everywhere.

He was in the faces of the children
As they played in the park and in their backyards.

He was in the wind as it tickled the leaves
While playing in and out of the branches of the trees.

He was in the stares of the elderly
As they replayed their days of Skip-a-Rope.

He was in the scamper of the squirrels as they
Played tag up and down the spruce trees.

He was in the clouds as they lazily drifted
Away after playing Peek-a-Boo with the sun.

He was in the flying and crawling insects
As they played hide-and-seek in the tall grass.

He was within me today as I walked purposefully;
Playing pressures of an ordinary day on my mind.

I searched for God and found him playing.
He was everywhere.

Now and every day—he'll be here
In the knowing smile playing on my lips.

Source Connection Affirmations

1. My body, mind, and soul are empowered by the knowledge that connecting with universal source allows me to grow emotionally, physically, and spiritually.
2. My body, mind, and soul commit to receiving unconditional love from source.
3. My body, mind, and soul release all previous beliefs that have kept me disconnected from source.
4. My body, mind, and soul receive confirmation every day that God is present in my life.
5. My body, mind, and soul trust in the knowledge that I am always taken care of.
6. My body, mind, and soul have learned that I am worthy and deserving of having God in my life.
7. My body, mind, and soul are accustomed to the feelings of love and joy, which radiate from source.
8. In acknowledging God, I enhance all aspects of my life.
9. My body, mind, and soul believe God is always there for me.
10. My body, mind, and soul acknowledge the beauty of all life.
11. My body, mind, and soul trust in the power of an unconditionally loving spiritual being.
12. I connect to source, raising my vibration and freeing my body, mind, and soul from the constraints of dis-empowering beliefs.

> **There is always power. If you are not standing in yours, you may have given it away.**

My energy is at its highest point during the times when I am totally at ease with my self-identity. A situation in which I feel the expectation to be anyone other than me describes the "web" I have built around my true self, while my illusionary character stands outside it. I realise that the feelings of inadequacy and self-devaluation create this network of lies. When I am not standing in my power, someone else has it.

At one time, not knowing who I was, it felt okay to pretend I was whoever other people wanted me to be. Once I began to know myself, it just wasn't acceptable anymore.

It is interesting to see the different people who move in and out of your life as your power grows. The vibrations you send out are a manifestation of your self-awareness. When you can be manipulated, manipulative people appear; when you are empowered, the people who are empowered themselves or are attracted to the idea of empowerment materialise.

If you are no longer influenced by other people's judgements, you have freed yourself from the restrictions of prejudices, both theirs and yours.

There is no one way you have to be or not be. There is only the way you are. That does not mean you cannot change; it simply means that you will determine when and if those changes are imminent and to what degree they will occur, if at all. The decisions will be based upon what you want out of your life, not what someone else feels will benefit you or them.

The web disappears when the false impression you portray to the world evaporates and there is only the authentic personality standing there.

Ask a child who is real and who is putting on an act. They know.

My granddaughter, who was eight years old at that time, was describing a friend of hers to me during a conversation several years ago. I remember her words clearly, as I was very impressed with her perspective. She said, "She is just a friend, Grandma, but not a real friend." When prompted, she explained, "When I play with her, she sometimes leaves me to play with someone else."

Are you a real friend to yourself? Or do you abandon your true self for another's perceptions of your identity?

The Web

When I allow myself to be me,
The fears disappear
As the self emerges from this web
I put myself in.
I cover myself with lies
When I choose to please others:
But then, I am unfaithful to myself.
I agree when I disagree,
I say yes when I mean no.
Choosing to be acceptable to another,
I become unacceptable to myself.
My truth lies beneath what others see.
I encourage their indifference,
Allowing their perception to influence me.
As my shadow self emerges,
I realise I am never more alone;
Than when I am with people
Who don't know who I am!

Power Affirmations

1. My body, mind, and soul release fear as I move into my power.
2. My power increases as I expand my belief in myself.
3. As I move into my power, my body, mind, and soul celebrate.
4. In taking back my power, I allow myself to become whole.
5. My body, mind, and soul realise that being in my power is my right.
6. In accepting myself, my body, mind, and soul are freed from limitation.
7. When in my power, my body, mind, and soul connect as one.
8. My body, mind, and soul are empowered by the knowledge that my being is enhanced when I retain my power.
9. My body, mind, and soul recognise the importance of staying in my power.
10. My body, mind, and soul trust in my journey and the contribution I make as an enlightened being.
11. My body, mind, and soul understand that in embracing my power I renew my commitment to myself.
12. My body, mind, and soul realise I have support on every step of my journey.

> **Search your soul for purpose in your life.**
> **The revealing moment brings with it a passion,**
> **which opens a flow of confirming opportunities.**

Purpose gives you a passion for life. Possibilities open up, which you may not have previously considered.

When I was younger and seemingly on a path to self-destruction, I was not only disconnected from source but without purpose. Searching for meaning in my life, I felt rejected by others. An essential piece of my life was missing, and looking back at it now from a different perspective allows me to evaluate my experiences from that time. There were certain expectations I felt I had to meet then, many of which didn't feel right for me.

Once I became a wife and mother, I tried hard to make everything perfect on the outside but felt trapped inside. It was of my own making, as I was the one who didn't let anyone see the real me. Everything was for someone else—my family, my teachers, my young students and their parents, and even for my egotistical self—but my authentic core was virtually ignored.

Once I realised my soul felt unfulfilled, I made fulfilment my purpose and passionately set out to achieve it. Everything changed that moment. I was now on course. Obstacles fell away as any limits I once had were erased. Life began to flow. Opportunities that I would have been afraid to take before opened up as I followed my heart.

Now realising my experiences are a part of who I am, I am grateful for all of them and feel blessed every day for the people in my life. There are no regrets—only accomplishments—as everything has led me here.

Figuring out what is missing in your life, whether it is joy, love, trust, or whatever else it may be, is a good first step to finding direction in your life. It doesn't have to take anything away from others; in fact, it may add to their lives as well as your being will resonate with purpose. When you love yourself and what you are doing, that love extends out to others.

Purpose

The flowers, trees, grass, and sky
Have a purpose; as do I.
Life is meant to be lived
With all the passion you have to give.

Bare feet on—run outside,
Your life is yours to decide.
No more holding yourself in
The time is now—so begin.

Yell to the sky; let the universe hear
How you aspire to know no fear.
Acknowledge your truth for a start,
Then feel free to follow your heart.

Once you're ready, you will find
The life you've celebrated in your mind.
What once you thought was concealed,
Is now open—your purpose revealed.

Purpose Affirmations

1. My body, mind, and soul believe in the power of purpose.
2. In pursuing purpose, my body, mind, and soul resonate with life.
3. The ability to find purpose comes from my body, mind, and soul's passion for life.
4. My body, mind, and soul expel fear as I move toward my purpose.
5. My body, mind, and soul embrace my purpose, knowing it transforms my life positively.
6. Acknowledging the truth of who I am allows my body, mind, and soul to live a purposeful life.
7. My body, mind, and soul claim my right to live in purpose.
8. My body, mind, and soul accept the spiritual freedom that my purpose provides.
9. My body, mind, and soul commit to my purpose, embracing the knowledge that it fulfils me.
10. My body, mind, and soul receive confirmation that I am on my path.
11. My body, mind, and soul believe in the power of a purposeful life.
12. My body, mind, and soul are grateful for the energy of purpose in my life, recognising it as an essential part of my journey.

> # Fear's limiting capabilities prevent you
> # from stepping into your life.

Fear is the illusion that holds us in place. It is the ego's way of keeping us safe and diminishes the ability to fully step into life and appreciate the potential we all have. Holding on to this false impression of security brings another side effect: the lack of courage to change or move forward.

I have lived in fear the majority of my life. It has prevented me from achieving my goals and changing my life until now, but not from perceived harm. I still experienced episodes of sexual, physical, and verbal abuse, feelings of inadequacy, severed relationships, survived deaths of loved ones, and more.

This false sense of security that has kept me from exploring possibilities and opportunities has limited more than protected me. The impact of this insight has allowed me to reconsider many former beliefs and decisions. The book you are reading, for instance, would never have been written if I had, once again, succumbed to fear.

I have been interested in writing most of my life and only recently let go of feelings of insecurity around releasing personal information to others. With the realisation that liberating myself from fear not only can help me but others too is an added incentive to letting go. As we are all connected, the more we help ourselves, the more everyone benefits.

With the feeling of universal love and acceptance comes the understanding that there is nothing to fear. Your ability to accomplish anything is enhanced because there is nothing to stop you.

When I began teaching spiritual workshops a few years ago, a friend of mine that I hadn't seen in years but who knew me prior to the changes I had made in my life made a comment about how she always wondered about the lives of the spiritually aware. She was aspiring to be at the same place in her life as them without fully realising that many of them probably had their own share of difficulties to overcome as well.

We are all on a journey, and everybody starts somewhere. Wherever you are now is the perfect place to begin.

Never Afraid

I walk on the edge of the cliff,
And I am not afraid.
Your love holds me fast on the trail.

I fly to the end of all within my vision,
And I am not afraid.
Your love gives me unlimited sight.

I sink to the cold, dark depths,
And I am not afraid.
Your warm love brings me to the surface.

I dream in the darkness of night,
And I am not afraid.
Your light radiates within me.

I live amidst confusion and judgement,
And I am never afraid.
Your acceptance empowers me!

Fear Affirmations

1. My body, mind, and soul are free to move forward from limiting beliefs, which have kept me from advancing on my path.
2. In the places of my body, mind, and soul where I have been fearful, I release these fears and allow myself to trust universal love.
3. I forgive my body, mind, and soul for believing that holding on to fear helps me.
4. I enable my body, mind, and soul to create freedom from fear.
5. My body, mind, and soul release all judgements around incidents that I feel have defined me.
6. My body, mind, and soul know that fear is debilitating, and in embracing the lessons I have learned from fearful incidents, I am now free from past limitations.
7. Acknowledging that fear is an illusion, my body, mind, and soul embrace my full potential.
8. My body, mind, and soul see unlimited possibilities and opportunities before me.
9. All the insecurities in my mind, body, and soul resulting from fear-based thoughts are now extinct, allowing me full access to my future.
10. My body, mind, and soul are committed to receiving unlimited opportunities.
11. I open my, body, mind, and soul unlimited access to freeing thoughts.
12. My body, mind, and soul release fear and realise the abundance of universal love.

> **When you release the shadows, clarity frees you to begin.**

The constant presence of animals in my life is an inspiration to me. As I have mentioned earlier, birds are especially prevalent in my life. Having had many unusual experiences with these divine messengers, several of them involving ravens, I have learned to love and appreciate this bird. From a physical angle, many people have said they find ravens mischievous and annoying, but metaphysically, I see in them an intelligence and knowing beyond my comprehension.

My first experience with animal spirit totems was when one of my co-workers—who is, incidentally, blind yet very insightful—told me she saw a raven with me. Immediately sensing the connection, my communication with Raven began that moment. From then on, I spoke to Raven and it to me.

Raven showed me that my understanding of existence is quite limited and encouraged me to open up to more possibilities. It also told me that being a natural healer, I was capable of so much more than I had ever given myself credit for.

When I began working with clients, even though many of them came to me with physical or emotional issues, I noticed that they were actually searching for soul connection. Though I had never thought of myself as a spiritual counsellor before, it has now become an important quality of my work with others. Now, in any workshop I teach, the spiritual aspect is present as are animal helpers, since Raven has a unique connection to all beings.

Raven has led me from being a novice seeker of truth to where I am now: letting go of old paradigms, accepting a new reality, and embracing opportunities that take me into formerly unknown territory. It has taught me self-acceptance and a new way of looking at magic, as well as an appreciation of the alchemy within every one of us.

Listen: Raven Speaks

Before Raven spoke to me,
I was afraid and in the dark;
Wanted light—didn't know how to start.
Through the shadows, I couldn't see;
Before Raven spoke to me.

Before Raven spoke to me
I held my voice, hesitant to grow;
Wanted to speak—kept the volume low.
Through the shadows, I couldn't see;
Before Raven spoke to me.

Before Raven spoke to me
I was lost, helpless, and weak;
Wanted strength—felt too meek.
Through the shadows, I couldn't see;
Before Raven spoke to me.

Before Raven spoke to me,
I drummed alone, music lost too soon;
Wanted harmony—felt out of tune.
Through the shadows, I couldn't see;
Before Raven spoke to me.

Now Raven speaks to me
Of my voice, strength, music, and light within;
Showed me the magic—freed me to begin.
There are no shadows, as I see—
Now that Raven speaks to me.

Possibility Affirmations

1. My body, mind, and soul open up to possibilities I have not previously been aware of.
2. My body, mind, and soul accept the possibilities that enhance my journey.
3. In my body, mind, and soul, I realise all things are possible.
4. I forgive my body, mind, and soul for believing in only what I physically see.
5. My body, mind, and soul eradicate any previous beliefs in which I was not accepting of abundance because of my need to understand all I embrace.
6. I enhance my body, mind, and soul's journey through acceptance of all there can be, knowing impossibility is an illusion.
7. I permit my body, mind, and soul to receive messages that enhance my growth on all levels.
8. In accepting what I once thought was impossible, my body, mind, and soul embrace endless perspectives.
9. My body, mind, and soul believe that all I am comes from the possibilities I embrace.
10. My body, mind, and soul welcome all possibilities I once thought impossible.
11. My body, mind, and soul trust in the endless alchemy of the universe's magic.
12. When I believe all things are possible, they are.

> ## The image you present to the world is a reflection of your self-perception.

When meditating outdoors, I gain profound appreciation of everything around me. Being in nature unlocks a door and invites me to look beyond the superficial and delve deeper into life. It seems as if Mother Earth opens up her arms to me, gives me a hug, and provides an easel on which to paint my thoughts. A different perspective is available when observing everything in its natural environment.

The following poem entitled "Reflections" is a result of one of those beautiful, solitary days in which the illusion of limits in my life dissolved while I contemplated nature and my connection with it.

My thoughts expanded to my own identity and the correlation I felt with the rest of the world. While questioning where I belonged and the impact each of us is able to make on others, the reflection of the trees on the water caught my attention, which allowed me to speculate on the images we present to the world and to ourselves each day. Every one of us is a ripple in the water of life, and we all contribute an important piece to the universal puzzle. The picture would not be complete without all the pieces.

The imprint we make on other people is a result of our own feelings of self-worth, self-respect, and self-love. We give what we have to give and nothing more. The more we give out, the more we will receive in return. This cycle of giving and receiving creates a circle of abundance for all. There truly is enough love, enough joy, enough of everything for everyone if we can find the trust within to give and the humbleness to receive.

Reflections

As I sit by the pond, I meditate on questions of life;
The water ripples as if in answer to the solutions I seek;
The trees reflect back an image I see as my soul—
Illuminating back to me the physical and spiritual aspects of self.
Am I as this image is?
Mirroring the physical aspects of self,
Revealing the soul when the time is right?
Creating an illusion that just touches the surface,
Holding the real self inside?
Or . . .
Do I continually present my image as the trees do on the water—
Seen only when someone pauses to look?

Facing my own reflection in the water,
I ask, "Am I all that I see,
Or am I the illusion I present to the rest of the world?"
In the end, I recognise I am both and neither.
I am my heart, I am what I desire, I am what I choose.

As I aim a pebble at my reflection, I realise the ripple I cause
reaches out;
Circling far beyond my image, like the rain that penetrates the
ground and disappears;
Or as the tree roots which spread down into the earth, leaving
only the evidence of the tree to prove their existence.

Do I, too, reach far beyond what I see and have the ability to
create a ripple?
Is this my ego or is it my truth?

These questions I ask; their answers I seek.
But . . . is it really for me to know?
If I create the illusion of myself, which conveys to others a sense
of belonging in this world, does it matter why?
As I sit by the pond, I again meditate on the questions of life.

Self-Perception Affirmations

1. My body, mind, and soul accommodate my perception of myself as a loving, caring human being.
2. My body, mind, and soul reflect the image that I am capable of loving myself and others.
3. In my body, mind, and soul, I acknowledge my perfection.
4. My body, mind, and soul create opportunities to express my true self.
5. In my body, mind, and soul, I recognise my contribution to the universe as essential.
6. Embracing my soul's identity, my body and mind project my awareness of my perfect self to others.
7. Expelling illusions of self from my body, mind, and soul allows me to connect with the world in truth and integrity.
8. My body, mind, and soul embrace humbling qualities that allow me to forgive myself and others.
9. I commit to loving myself in order to give love to others.
10. I allow my mind, body, and soul to be an integral piece in the circle of abundance.
11. The choices of my body, mind, and soul are reflected in the abundance of peace, joy, and love being returned to me.
12. My body, mind, and soul trust in the knowledge that all I give out will come back to me in greater quantities than I remitted.

> **When you only see the cocoon, limits block you; but perceiving the distinguishing outline of the butterfly is liberating.**

The butterfly has long been a symbol of change because of its transformation from a chrysalis to a mature state. Every time I see this beautiful creature, it reminds me of the many changes I have gone through in my life. Many of my day-by-day experiences did not have as much of an impact as those which the universe sent to me as an awakening because I wasn't paying attention for the first, second, and third time.

Learning to look at the smallest incident as a powerful message rather than waiting for stronger communication methods that are too forceful to ignore, I am able to see my sense of balance, harmony, and peace as a reflection of the perceptions I possess. And when I am not holding the ideal of my perfection, the universe conspires to call it to my attention. My gratitude for these reminders is infinite, and even though they sometimes hurt, the realisation that they are given to me to enhance my growth compels me to persevere, knowing that universal love is behind their emergence.

As long as there is life, there is growth. So although the lessons still arrive, I have learned to deal with them in a more positive, timely manner so contact is less intense but wisdom prevails.

Having resources such as Deep Cellular Healing and Reiki are a big help, and I use these methods faithfully. They, along with amazing, supportive and wise people in my life have helped me to become balanced, to trust, to give and accept love, to have joy, to live in purpose and release fear.

My astute daughter once said to me when we were learning to ski a few years ago: "I don't think I learned anything today, I didn't fall once." How many times have you fallen today and how hard are you willing to land?

Life Changes

I just saw the butterfly!
What does that mean to me?
Oh! Freedom!
Freedom to change;
Freedom to be me;
Freedom to speak my truth;
Freedom to move forward;
Freedom to follow my dreams.
Once, I only saw the cocoon.
Now, I am free to see the butterfly!

Awareness Affirmations

1. I allow my body, mind, and soul to accept universal awareness.
2. My body, mind, and soul understand that there is meaning in all my experiences.
3. My body, mind, and soul embrace awareness in new unlimited ways.
4. Awareness comes to me in forms that my body, mind, and soul recognise so I am guided in a gentle manner.
5. In my awareness, I am able to make choices that reflect my body, mind, and soul's best interests.
6. When I believe and trust in the universe, my body, mind, and soul rejoice.
7. Embracing awareness empowers my body, mind, and soul.
8. The knowledge that I am learning keeps my body, mind, and soul attuned to the gentle reminders in my life.
9. My body, mind, and soul choose awareness over ignorance, understanding that where I am right now is the ideal place to begin.
10. My body, mind, and soul remember that the times I fall are the opportune times to learn how to get up.
11. I expel any thoughts around failure from my body, mind, and soul, knowing that success comes from the learning of lessons.
12. My body, mind, and soul believe in my ability to receive balance and harmony through universal guidance.

> **Keep your light shining; you never know when someone is looking for a way out of the darkness.**

I adopted the image of the lighthouse as a logo for my business a while ago. The concept reflects being available for all, and this allegory is exactly what I want to portray to those searching to make changes in their lives.

The light, ever shining
Never wavers in its quest
To be of help to all who seek.

To be as the lighthouse is to stand still in one place so you can be found by anyone who seeks your assistance. It exemplifies staying solid, grounded, and bright enough so those who seek will be able to find you in the darkness.

I believe the Universe, God, Higher Power, or whatever name you choose to call the divine spirit, is the highest form of light. That unconditional loving light that forever shines is never farther than a prayer away.

Everyone has the potential to be an inspiration to someone. You never know when your light will be the beacon that invites a person in and encourages the change that makes the difference between a life lived in love or rooted in fear.

If you had forgotten how bright your light shines and how far it extends, now is the time to remember.

Forever Shining

The lighthouse sits alone
Watching, waiting for those in need
Of its light, the peace it brings.

The light, ever shining
Never wavers in its quest
To be of help to all who seek.

On guard it stands
Forever in one place
To be easily found.

It doesn't reach out
To say, "I'll give you a hand."
But sits quietly solid.

And you know
When the time is right,
It is there, unendingly patient.

On guard it stands
Forever in one place
To be easily found.

If you decide the need
Of its strength is great,
Its wait over; it enfolds you.

Releasing again when asked.
Silently each day and night,
Forever shining its light.

On guard it stands
Forever in one place
To be easily found.

Waiting

I do not seek,
Nor do I find;
I wait for you
To make up your mind.

When you feel lonely,
Or can't take anymore,
I'll be here
On this craggy shore.

When you feel anger,
Or when you feel fear;
Look to this sandy beach
For I am here.

When you are frustrated,
Or unable to decide;
Here I'll stand
On this stony hillside.

I do not seek,
Nor do I find:
I'll be here waiting—
Waiting until you make up your mind.

Contributors

I would like to acknowledge the contributions of the following image authors in this book. The following images can be found at *www.dreamstime.com.*

Cover Photo—Marilyn Volan
Pages four—Addaphoto
       eight—Susan Currie
       twelve—Eti Swinford
       twenty one—Starblue
       thirty—Ivan Kmit
       forty—Jseens
       forty four and forty eight-Mlan
       fifty two—Steven Bourelle
       sixty eight and one hundred and two—Rolffimages
       seventy two—Guilu
       seventy six—Amabrao
       eighty eight—Jeff Halbach
       ninety three—Alptraum
       ninety eight—Konradbak
       one hundred and six—Iiya Meriin
       one hundred and ten—Robiskip
       one hundred and fourteen—Mirceau Costina
       one hundred and eighteen—Elena Ray
       one hundred and twenty two—Audines
       one hundred and twenty four—Amyld

*Images on pages sixteen, twenty six, thirty five, fifty six, sixty, sixty four, eighty, and eighty four as well as the authors' photos were graciously contributed by Cheryl A. Maurice.

Index

CPSIA information can be obtained
at www.ICGtesting.com
Printed in the USA
LVOW12s0407210416
484588LV00001B/32/P